# Kid's Box

## Activity Book 2

Caroline Nixon & Michael Tomlinson

CAMBRIDGE UNIVERSITY PRESS

# 1 Hello again!

  **Write.**

I'm Stella.

I'm Simon.

I'm Suzy.

She's ___Stella.___ He's _____ _____

I'm Mr Star.

I'm Mrs Star.

I'm Grandpa.

Hello, I'm Grandma Star. This is my family.

_____ _____ _____

## 2 Draw and write.

What's your name?

_____

How old are you?

_____

# Colour the stars.

**1**

Colour two stars.

**2**

Colour five stars.

**3**

Colour six stars.

**4**

Colour one star.

**5**

Colour eight stars.

  # Match and join.

| | | |
|---|---|---|
| **1** Three and one is … | ten | 3 |
| **2** One and two is … | four | 7 |
| **3** Five and three is … | seven | 4 |
| **4** Seven and two is … | eight | 9 |
| **5** Six and four is … | three | 8 |
| **6** Three and four is … | nine | 10 |

3

**Listen and colour.**

   **Write the words. Listen and correct.**

**1** This is __Stella__  She's __eight__

**2** This is _____  He's _____

**3** This is _____  She's _____

**7**  # Find the 'colour' words. Colour the stars.

| | | | |
|---|---|---|---|
| black | ★ | purple | ☆ |
| red | ☆ | blue | ☆ |
| yellow | ☆ | white | ☆ |
| pink | ☆ | grey | ☆ |
| green | ☆ | brown | ☆ |
| orange | ☆ | | |

```
o  r  a  n  g  e  w  a (b)
t  e  a  l  r  p  h  i  l
w  h  i  t  e  u  i  r  a
a  a  b  b  e  r  d  o  c
g  f  l  o  n  p  i  n  k
r  u  u  t  i  l  f  c  i
e  s  e  w  i  e  r  e  d
y  e  l  l  o  w  r  l  o
g  r  a  n  b  r  o  w  n
```

 **8**  # Match and colour.

| 7 grey | nine | 8 yellow | three | 5 pink |
|---|---|---|---|---|
| 6 blue | ten | two | 10 orange | four |
| five | 3 purple | 9 green | eight | 1 brown |
| 2 red | seven | six | 4 black | one |

5

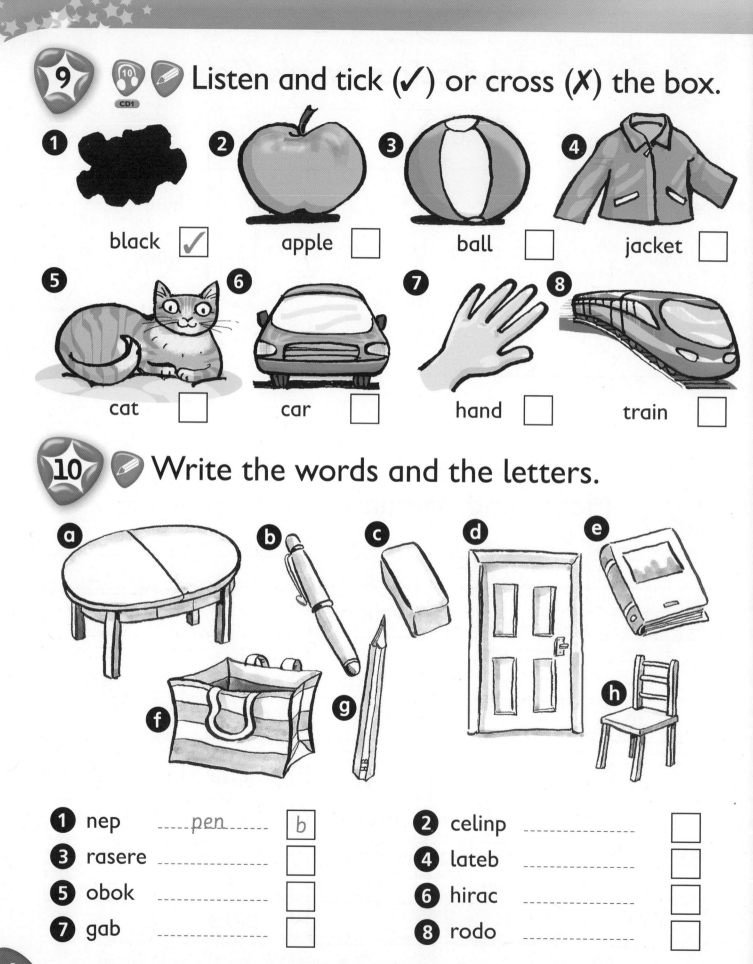

**9** 🎧 CD1 ✏️ Listen and tick (✔) or cross (✗) the box.

1 black ✔

2 apple ☐

3 ball ☐

4 jacket ☐

5 cat ☐

6 car ☐

7 hand ☐

8 train ☐

**10** ✏️ Write the words and the letters.

1 nep _____pen_____ | b |
3 rasere _____ ☐
5 obok _____ ☐
7 gab _____ ☐

2 celinp _____ ☐
4 lateb _____ ☐
6 hirac _____ ☐
8 rodo _____ ☐

## ★ My picture dictionary

| | | |
|---|---|---|
| black | purple | yellow |
| black | | |
| green | pink | blue |
| | | |

## ★ My progress ★

Tick (✓) or cross (✗).

I can count to ten. ☐

I can say the colours. ☐

I can say the alphabet. ☐

# 2 Back to school

## 1   Find and write the words.

desk

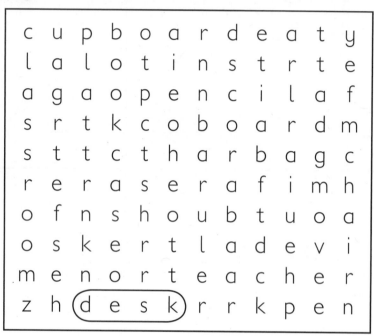

```
c u p b o a r d e a t y
l a l o t i n s t r t e
a g a o p e n c i l a f
s r t k c o b o a r d m
s t t c t h a r b a g c
r e r a s e r a f i m h
o f n s h o u b t u o a
o s k e r t l a d e v i
m e n o r t e a c h e r
z h (d e s k) r r k p e n
```

## 2   Listen and colour.

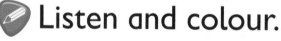

**Look at the numbers. Write the words.**

veleen
11

...eleven...

ewletv
12

----------

niffeet
15

----------

wytent
20

----------

hiegeetn
18

----------

reihtnet
13

----------

  **Read and colour.**

**17**

**19**

Colour number twelve brown.
Colour number nineteen pink.
Colour number fourteen green.
Colour number seventeen blue.
Colour number sixteen orange.

**16**

**14**

**12**

**5** 🎧 ✏️ **Listen and draw lines.**

**6** 🔍 ✏️ **Look and read. Write 'yes' or 'no'.**

**1** There are three teachers in the classroom. _____No._____

**2** There's a door next to the cupboard. _____Yes._____

**3** There's a board on the wall. _____

**4** There's a cupboard under the board. _____

**5** There are thirteen bags in the classroom. _____

**6** There are nineteen fish on the board. _____

**7** There are eighteen books in the bookcase. _____

**8** There's a ruler under the desk. _____

**9** There's a jacket on the chair. _____

**10** There's an orange on the table. _____

**1** ( a ruler ) ( There's ) ( the table. ) ( on )

**2** ( the desk. ) ( There are ) ( on ) ( 12 pencils )

**3** ( There's ) ( under ) ( the chair. ) ( a bag )

**4** ( the bookcase. ) ( 16 books ) ( in ) ( There are )

**1** There's a ruler on the table.

**2** _____

**3** _____

**4** _____

**8**  **Look at the picture. Write the answers.**

**1** How many burgers are there?  There are six.

**2** How many apples are there?  _____

**3** How many oranges are there?  _____

**4** How many cakes are there?  _____

**5** How many ice creams are there?  _____

**6** How many bananas are there?  _____

**Listen and find the different sound.**

a   b<u>i</u>g          <s>t<u>i</u>ger</s>        p<u>i</u>nk

b   f<u>i</u>ve         f<u>i</u>sh          k<u>i</u>tchen

c   s<u>i</u>ng         h<u>i</u>s           <u>i</u>ce cream

d   tr<u>ai</u>n        <u>i</u>n            s<u>i</u>x

e   g<u>i</u>raffe      b<u>ir</u>d          sw<u>i</u>m

f   g<u>ui</u>tar       p<u>i</u>cture       sk<u>ir</u>t

   **Find the words.**

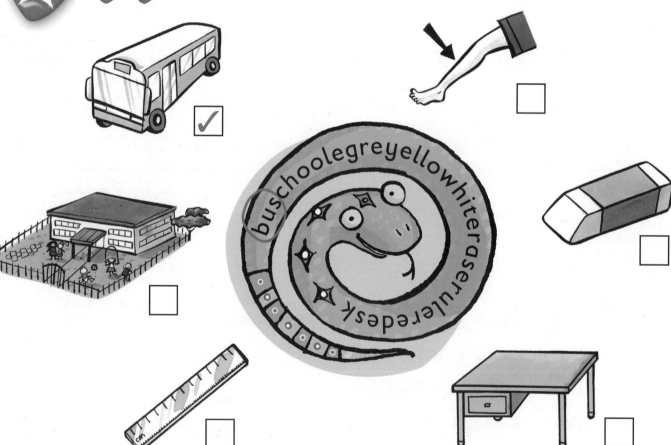

How many colours are there? _____

What are they? _____

# My picture dictionary

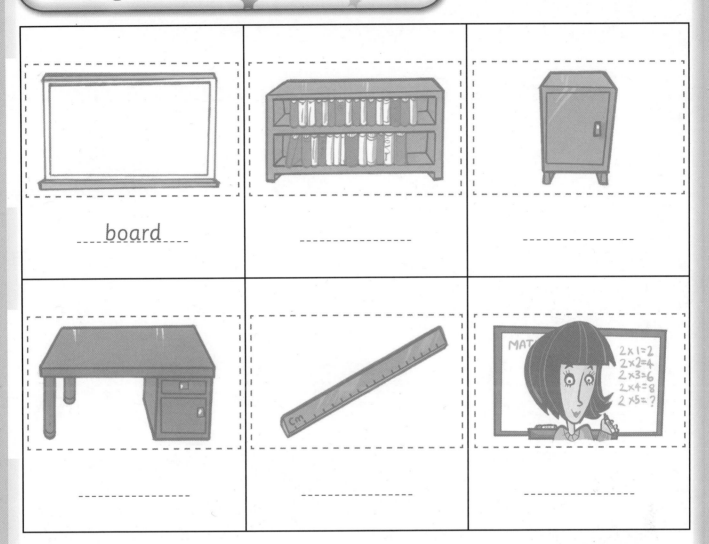

board

_____

_____

_____

_____

_____

# My progress

## Tick (✓) or cross (✗).

I can talk about my classroom. ☐

I can say the numbers 11–20. ☐

I can spell. ☐

# 3 Play time!

## 1   Read. Circle the toy words. Write.

_ _ _ _ _ _ _ _ _ _ _ _ _ _ _ _ _ _ _ _ _ _ _ _ _ _ _ _ _

_ _ _ _ _

Suzy's got a (kite) and a doll. Simon's got a robot and a lorry. Lenny's got a train and a monster. Meera's got an orange camera and a car. Stella's got a computer game. Alex has got a big yellow watch and a bike.

_ _ _ _ _ _ _

_ _ _ _ 　　k i t e 　　_ _ _ _ _ 　　_ _ _ _ _ _ _

## 2  Listen and tick (✓) the box.

**1** **a**  ✓ 　 **b** 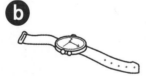 ☐ 　 **c**  ☐

**2** **a**  ☐ 　 **b**  ☐ 　 **c**  ☐

**3** **a**  ☐ 　 **b**  ☐ 　 **c**  ☐

**4** **a**  ☐ 　 **b**  ☐ 　 **c**  ☐

**Complete the sentences and colour the pictures.**

1. __This__ is a red __plane__
2. __These__ are purple __watches__
3. _____ are blue _____
4. _____ is a brown _____
5. _____ are green _____
6. _____ are grey _____
7. _____ are yellow _____
8. _____ are blue _____

**Match. Write the words.**

d _____ _____doll_____ _____dog_____

ca _____ _____ _____

tr _____ _____ _____

kit _____ _____ _____

pl _____ _____ _____

r _____ _____ _____

~~og~~

ke

ane

~~oll~~

mera

ain

ease

chen

uler

ousers

e

obot

15

**5** 🎧 34 CD1 ✏️ Listen and colour.

a  b  c  d  e  f

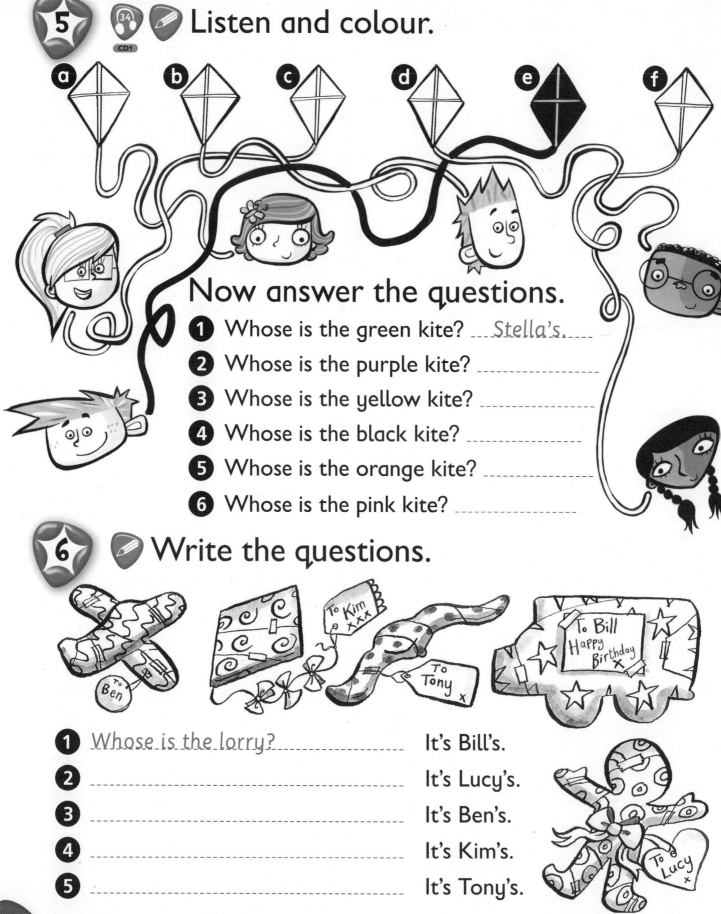

## Now answer the questions.

**1** Whose is the green kite? _____Stella's._____

**2** Whose is the purple kite? _____

**3** Whose is the yellow kite? _____

**4** Whose is the black kite? _____

**5** Whose is the orange kite? _____

**6** Whose is the pink kite? _____

**6** ✏️ Write the questions.

**1** _Whose is the lorry?_____ It's Bill's.

**2** _____ It's Lucy's.

**3** _____ It's Ben's.

**4** _____ It's Kim's.

**5** _____ It's Tony's.

# Choose and join.

Nick      Sam      Ann      Jill

# Now ask and join.

Whose is the robot?

It's Nick's.

Nick      Sam      Ann      Jill

**Tick (✓) or cross (✗) the box.**

| Where? | Who? | Watch |
|---|---|---|
|  ✓ | | |
| What? | Ear | White |
| | | |

  **Listen and join the dots.**

6 •

14 •

3 •

5 •

2 •

17 •

19 •

1 •

10 •

8 •    11 •    13 •  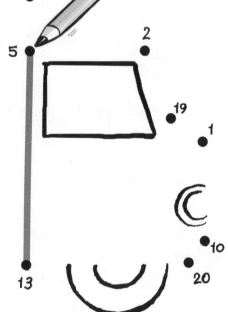  20 •

**What is it?    It's a _____ .**

## ★ My picture dictionary

camera

_____

_____

_____

_____

_____

## ★ My progress

### Tick (✓) or cross (✗).

I can talk about my favourite toy. ☐

I can write 'toy' words. ☐

19

# 4 At home

## 1 🎧 42 CD1 ✏️ Listen and draw lines.

## 2 ✏️ Write the words.

Across →

Down ↓

2 l a m p

20

# 3 Write the numbers.

1. Thirteen and three is _sixteen_ = m
2. Nine and three is _____ = s
3. Twelve and two is _____ = l
4. Six and eleven is _____ = r
5. Fifteen and five is _____ = p
6. Six and twelve is _____ = o
7. Fourteen and five is _____ = f
8. Ten and three is _____ = i
9. Twelve and three is _____ = a

## Now write the words and draw.

1.

| m |  |  |  |  |  |
|---|---|---|---|---|---|
| 16 | 13 | 17 | 17 | 18 | 17 |

2.

|  |  |  |  |
|---|---|---|---|
| 14 | 15 | 16 | 20 |

3.

|  |  |  |  |
|---|---|---|---|
| 12 | 18 | 19 | 15 |

# 4 Read and write the words.

| phone   ~~mirror~~   sofa   mat   armchair |

1. You can see your face in it. ____mirror____

2. Four children can sit on it. _____

3. It's small. It's got numbers. You can talk to your friend on it.

_____

4. One child can sit on it. _____

5. You can clean your shoes on it. _____

**5** Write 'yours' or 'mine'.

**1** Whose is this?
It's __mine__.

**2** Is this _____ or Simon's?
It's mine.

**3** Is this _____?
Yes, it is.

**4** Whose are these?
They're _____.

 **6**  Listen and colour.

22

**7**  Write 'his' or 'hers'.

**1** The long ruler is _hers._

**2** The big bag is _____

**3** The white jacket is _____

**4** The grey jacket is _____

**5** The clean shoes are _____

**6** The short ruler is _____

**7** The dirty shoes are _____

**8** The small bag is _____

 **8** Write the letters and the words. Tick (✓) the pictures.

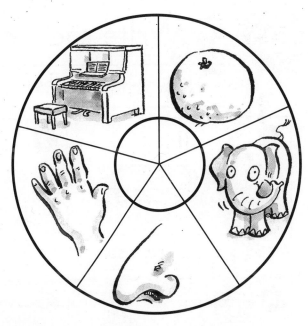

_ _ n _ _ _ _            _ _ _ _ _ _

 ☐   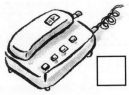 ☐    ☐    ☐    ☐

**Read and draw lines.** ↓ ↘ →

**1**

| which | where | white |
|-------|-------|-------|
| boat | whose | one |
| window | wall | book |

**2**

| kitchen | child | his |
|---------|-------|-----|
| swim | skirt | kite |
| guitar | write | this |

**3**

| cat | face | lamp |
|-----|------|------|
| chair | man | black |
| hand | are | ball |

**4**

| leg | read | desk |
|-----|------|------|
| her | bed | see |
| ear | feet | head |

  **Write the words.**

| This | That | These | Those | These | That |
|------|------|-------|-------|-------|------|

**1** That is a sofa.

**2** _____ is a phone.

**3** _____ are armchairs.

**4** _____ is a clock.

**5** _____ are mats.

**6** _____ are beds.

# My picture dictionary

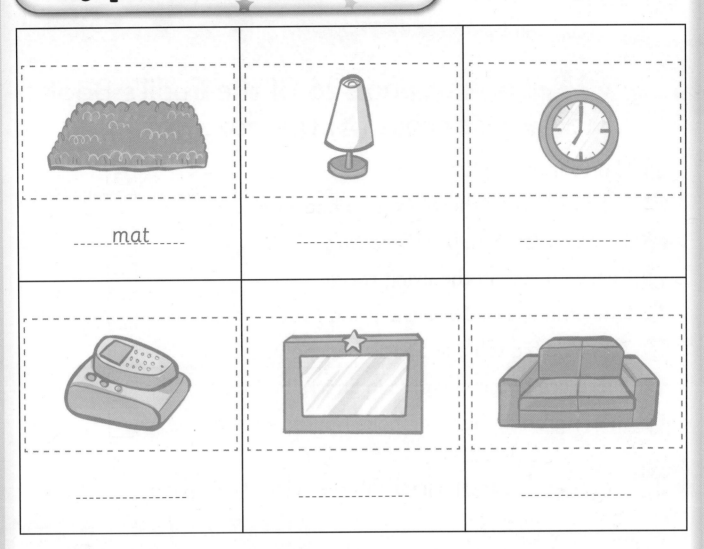

mat

_____

_____

_____

_____

_____

# My progress

## Tick (✓) or cross (✗).

I can talk about my house. ☐

I can say what's mine. ☐

25

# Our world

**1**  Look at page 26 of the Pupil's Book. Tick (✓) or cross (✗) the box.

1. Shari's from England. ✗
2. In Shari's house there are two bedrooms. ☐
3. There's a kitchen, but there isn't a hall. ☐
4. There's a sofa in the living room. ☐
5. Shari can watch TV in the living room. ☐
6. There's a big table in Shari's bedroom. ☐
7. There are two cupboards in Shari's bedroom. ☐
8. Shari's grandfather can make houses with snow. ☐

**2** 54 CD1 Listen and write the number.

 ☐
 ☐
 ☐

 13
 ☐
 ☐

# 3  Write the questions. Answer the questions.

|   | a | b | c | d | e | f |
|---|---|---|---|---|---|---|
| 1 | what | lorries | dirty | how | big | bed |
| 2 | shoes | toy | clean | small | balls | whose |
| 3 | is | small | camera | many | are | chair |
| 4 | there | under | where | on | the | or |

**1** 4c 3e 4e 1b

*Where are the lorries?* _____ ?

_____

**2** 2f 2b 3a 4d 4e 1f

_____ ?

**3** 3e 4e 2a 2c 4f 1c

_____ ?

_____

**4** 1d 3d 1b 3e 4a

_____ ?

**5** 4c 3a 4e 3c

_____ ?

_____

**6** 1a 3a 4d 4e 3f

_____ ?

_____

**Read and write the names.**

This is Lenny and his family. He's with his brother Sam, his sister May, and his cousin Frank. Lenny's brother has got a big nose. Lenny has got small eyes. Lenny's cousin is young. He's a baby. Lenny's sister has got long hair.

  **Write the words.**

~~sofa~~  ~~mummy~~  ~~plane~~  ~~bookcase~~  teacher  grandma  baby
kite  desk  lorry  grandpa  playground  cousin  bath  robot
board  mirror  boat  lamp  daddy  bed  ruler  doll  phone

| In the house | Family | Toys | At school |
|---|---|---|---|
| *sofa* | *mummy* | *plane* | *bookcase* |

-------------------- -------------------- -------------------- --------------------

Hello. This is my family. My mummy's got long purple hair, small green ears and five yellow teeth. Her name's Trudy. My daddy's name's Tom. He's got short red hair and a dirty green nose. He's got eight brown teeth. My brother Tony's got long brown hair, big red eyes and one white tooth. My sister's name is Tricia. She's very clean! She's got big ears, short blue hair, orange eyes and six green teeth.

**4**  **Write the words.**

( bbya )  ( afntharedrg )  ( anthmoredrg )  ( oremth )

( sstire )  ( fthrea )  ( ddyda )  ( csinou )  ( rthbore )  ( ymmmu )

  ........ *baby* ........

........................
........................
........................
........................
........................

  ........ *baby* ........

........................
........................
........................
........................
........................

29

**Write the letters.**

**1** What are you doing, Mum? ☐ i

**2** What are you drawing, Grandma? ☐

**3** Whose shoes are you cleaning, Grandpa? ☐

**4** Whose kite are you flying, Simon? ☐

**5** What are you eating, Dad? ☐

**6** Which word are you spelling, Stella? ☐

**7** I'm eating chocolate ice cream. ☐

**8** I'm drawing Stella. ☐

**9** I'm flying your kite, Suzy. ☐

**10** I'm making a cake. ☐

**11** I'm spelling 'beautiful'. ☐

**12** I'm cleaning Simon's shoes. ☐

   **Listen and correct.**

**Write the 'food' words.**

**Down ↓**

1

2

4

5

**Across →**

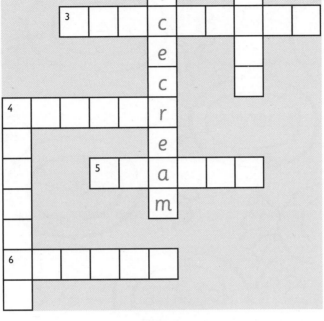
3

4

6

Crossword grid:
¹i
³_ _ _   c   _   ²_ _
e
c
⁴_ _ _ _ _   r
e
⁵_   a   _ _ _
m
⁶_ _ _ _ _

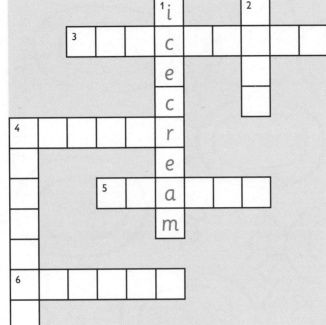 **Now complete the sentences.**

1 ↓ He's eating an *ice cream.*

2 ↓ They're _____ _____

3 → She's _____ _____

4 → He's _____ a _____

4 ↓ _____ _____ _____

5 → _____ an _____

6 → _____ _____ _____

31

## 8 ✏️ Colour the pairs.

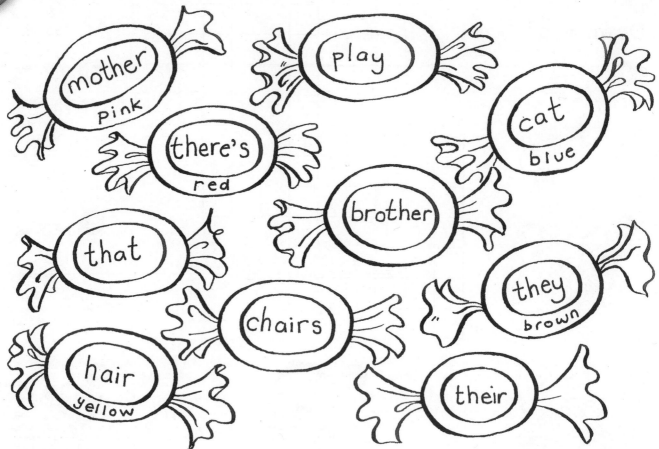

## 9 ✏️ Write the letters.

| | | | |
|---|---|---|---|
| a | He's kicking | her car. | |
| b | They're cleaning | in her bed. | |
| c | He's cleaning | a football. | a |
| d | She's sleeping | books. | |
| e | We're singing | a song. | |
| f | I'm playing | the guitar. | |
| g | She's driving | their teeth. | |
| h | They're reading | his shoes. | |

# My picture dictionary

mummy

# My progress

## Tick (✓) or cross (✗).

I can talk about my family. ☐

I can talk about actions. ☐

33

# 6 Dinner time

**1**  Read the lists and find the food.

Draw lines with a pencil.

Draw lines with a pen.

**a** Shopping list
- oranges
- bread
- rice
- bananas
- apples
- milk
- ice cream
- burgers
- apple juice
- eggs
- water

**b** Shopping list
- potatoes
- rice
- bread
- carrots
- fish
- orange juice
- chips
- chicken
- lemons
- meat

A Start

B Start

B Finish

A Finish

**2**  Find and colour.

Colour the pears green.
Colour the carrots orange.
Colour the tomatoes red.

Colour the chicken brown.
Colour the meat red.
Colour the lemons yellow.

**3** Draw and write about your favourite food. Ask and answer.

My favourite food is _____

_____

_____

_____

_____

**Listen and tick (✓) or cross (✗) the box.**

1. ✗
2. 
3. 
4. 

  **Read and write the numbers.**

Here you are. ☐

Can I have some juice, please? 1

Orange juice, please. ☐

Which juice – orange juice or apple juice? ☐

Which fruit – a banana, a pear or an apple? ☐

Here you are. ☐

Can I have some fruit, please? ☐

A pear, please. ☐

# 6 ✏ Choose. Tick (✓) the boxes.

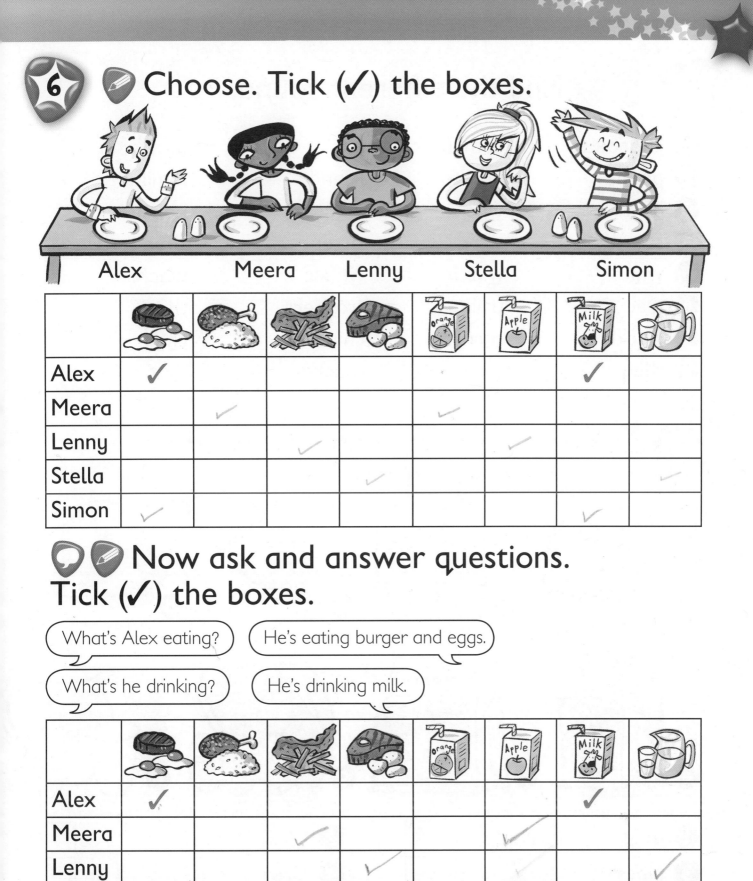

|  | 🍳 | 🍗 | 🍟 | 🐟 | Orange | Apple | Milk | 🥛 |
|---|---|---|---|---|---|---|---|---|
| Alex | ✓ |  |  |  |  |  | ✓ |  |
| Meera |  | ✓ |  |  | ✓ |  |  |  |
| Lenny |  |  | ✓ |  |  | ✓ |  |  |
| Stella |  |  |  | ✓ |  |  |  | ✓ |
| Simon | ✓ |  |  |  |  |  | ✓ |  |

## 💬 ✏ Now ask and answer questions. Tick (✓) the boxes.

What's Alex eating?    He's eating burger and eggs.

What's he drinking?    He's drinking milk.

|  | 🍳 | 🍗 | 🍟 | 🐟 | Orange | Apple | Milk | 🥛 |
|---|---|---|---|---|---|---|---|---|
| Alex | ✓ |  |  |  |  |  | ✓ |  |
| Meera |  |  | ✓ |  |  | ✓ |  |  |
| Lenny |  |  |  | ✓ |  | ✓ |  | ✓ |
| Stella |  | ✓ |  |  |  |  |  | ✓ |
| Simon |  |  | ✓ |  | ✓ |  |  |  |

**Find the different sound.**

1 ~~chocolate~~     computer     car     kite
2 phone     potato     friend     family
3 how     who     what     house
4 six     skirt     sister     shoe
5 white     watch     whose     where
6 tree     train     trousers     this
7 chicken     carrot     chips     chair
8 they     their     teacher     that

  **Write the words and the letters.**

1 gegs    _eggs_    `g`
2 lmki    ☐
3 pihcs    ☐
4 eirc    ☐
5 tarew    ☐
6 kiccehn    ☐
7 ceuji    ☐
8 radbe    ☐

# My picture dictionary

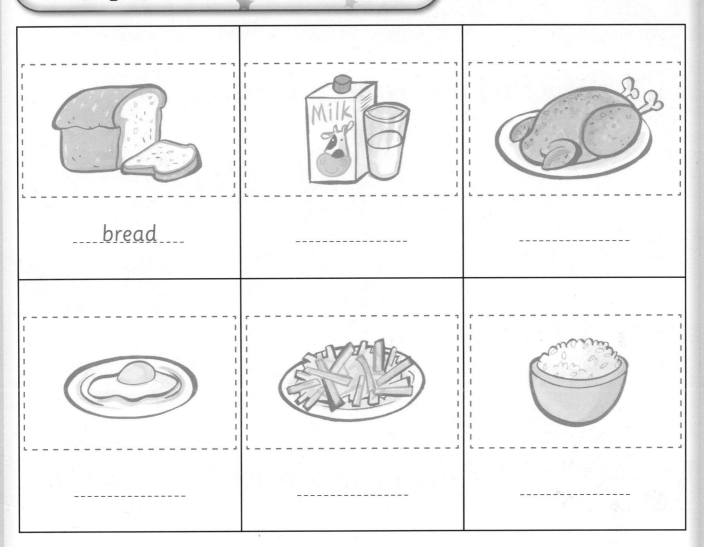

bread

# My progress

## Tick (✓) or cross (✗).

I can write 'food' words. ☐

I can talk about my favourite meal. ☐

I can ask about food. ☐

**1** Find and write the words.

| w | a | l | e | r | s | d | s | p | i |
|---|---|---|---|---|---|---|---|---|---|
| s | h | e | e | p | t | u | p | l | d |
| e | d | m | e | y | k | c | i | r | a |
| p | m | i | u | s | a | k | d | b | y |
| t | h | c | h | i | c | k | e | n | a |
| e | w | t | o | g | o | y | r | o | b |
| c | a | s | r | z | w | i | l | s | i |
| h | f | i | s | h | e | t | r | h | r |
| a | r | t | e | l | i | z | a | r | d |
| m | o | u | s | e | f | r | e | n | d |
| s | g | o | a | t | r | f | r | e | v |

horse

 **2** Read. Draw and write the words.

~~snakes~~   ~~crocodiles~~   fish   lizards   birds   giraffes   tigers   monkeys

This is the Star zoo. The birds are next to the snakes. The fish are under the birds. The lizards are between the fish and the monkeys. The yellow and brown animals next to the monkeys are giraffes. The big orange and black cats under the crocodiles are tigers.

snakes

crocodiles

**Choose and circle the animals.**

  **Now ask and circle the animals.**

How many cows are there?  There are six.

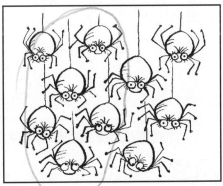

41

# Write the words. Listen and check.

| love | I | So | do | I | love | lizards | don't |

**1**

**a** I __love__ spiders.

**b** So do _____ .

**2**

**c** _____ love fish.

**d** _____ do I.

**3**

**e** I love _____ .

**f** So _____ I.

**4**

**g** I _____ goats.

**h** I _____ .

 # Draw your favourite animal and ask your friend.

What's your favourite animal?

I love _____

## 6    Find the words.

How many animals are there?

-----------------------------------------------------

What are they?

-----------------------------------------------------

-----------------------------------------------------

##  Now write the words.

t _ _ _ _ _ _ _

n _ _ _

g _ _ _

b e d

p _ _ _ _

s _ _ _ _ _

e _ _ _ _ _ _ _

d _ _ _

k _ _ _ _ _ _

e _ _

**7** Can you hear 'sh'? Tick (✓) or cross (✗) the box.

| 1 | 2 | 3 | 4 | 5 | 6 | 7 | 8 | 9 | 10 |
|---|---|---|---|---|---|---|---|---|----|
| ✓ |   |   |   |   |   |   |   |   |    |

**8**   Write the 'animal' words.

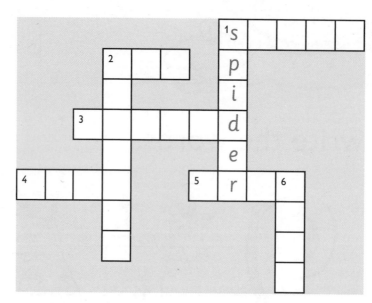

¹s p i d e r

**Down ↓**

**1** This is small and black. It's got eight legs.

**2** We can get eggs from this bird. It's brown or white.

**6** This farm animal has got a big body and a small head. It can eat clothes.

**Across →**

**1** This farm animal has got a big white body and a small head. It's got a short tail and a lot of hair.

**2** This big farm animal is brown and white or black and white. We can get milk from it.

**3** This animal is green or brown. It's got a long body and a small head. It's got four small feet and a long thin tail.

**4** This bird has got orange feet. It can swim.

**5** This small green animal can swim and jump. It's got big feet and long legs. It's got very big eyes and no ears.

44

# My picture dictionary

cow

_____

_____

_____

_____

_____

# My progress

Tick (✓) or cross (✗).

I can write 'animal' words. ☐

I can talk about things I love. ☐

45

# 8 My town

**1**  Look and read. Tick (✓) or cross (✗) the box.

 **1** This is a flat. ✗

 **2** This is a shop. ☐

 **3** This is a hospital. ☐

 **4** This is a street. ☐

 **5** This is a park. ☐

 **6** This is a café. ☐

**2**  Match. Write the words.

| | | |
|---|---|---|
| st | _street_ | _store_ |
| bo | ............ | ............ |
| ap | ............ | ............ |
| sh | ............ | ............ |
| p | ............ | ............ |
| ho | ............ | ............ |

reet

ple

use

otato

op

at

artment

oes

okshop

ore

spital

ark

## Spot the differences.

**1** In A there's one car, but in B there are two cars.

**2** .............................................................................................

**3** .............................................................................................

**4** .............................................................................................

**5** .............................................................................................

**6** .............................................................................................

 ## Write the words.

| ~~ball~~ ~~pear~~ ~~chair~~ ~~dog~~ coconut armchair table bike apple |
| computer game lizard pineapple cat train car lemon |
| lorry fish mouse painting clock orange bird cupboard |

**FRED'S FRUIT**
pear

**TED'S TOYS**
ball

**Pete's Pets**
dog

**Phil's Furniture**
chair

**Listen and colour the stars.**

 1     2     3

4    5    6

7    8    9

**6**   **Read and write the names.**

Tom

You're Tom. You're sitting in front of Jill.
You're Ann. You're sitting between Tom and Nick.
You're Bill. You're sitting behind Nick.
You're Sue. You're sitting between Jill and Bill.

## 7 ✏️ Choose and draw.

| in | on | next to | between | in front of | behind |
|---|---|---|---|---|---|

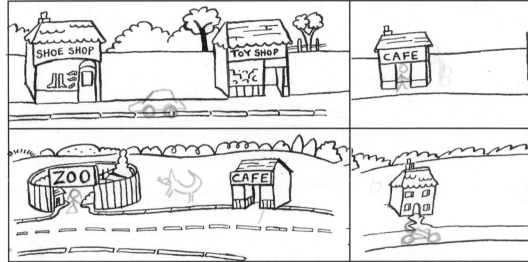

## 💬 ✏️ Now ask and draw.

Where's the car?    It's in front of the toy shop.

**8** **Read the words and draw lines.**

dog

box

goat

shop

nose

clock

no

boat

throw

sofa

sock

frog

  **9** **Draw a city. Write about it.**

The pet shop _____

The toy shop _____

The café _____

The hospital _____

The park _____

The flat _____

# My picture dictionary

park

_____

_____

_____

_____

_____

## My progress

Tick (✓) or cross (✗).

I can talk about the city. ☐

I can write about the city. ☐

**1** 🔍✏️ **Look at page 52 of the Pupil's Book. Write 'yes' or 'no'.**

1. Todd's from Australia. ...Yes...
2. Todd's house is in a city. ..........
3. Todd's mum and dad have got a pet shop. ..........
4. Todd's family have got a lot of cows. ..........
5. There are 12 dogs on their farm. ..........
6. The dogs run and get the sheep. ..........
7. Todd can't go to school. ..........
8. Todd can talk to his teacher on the computer. ..........
9. There's a big hospital next to Todd's house. ..........
10. A doctor can fly to Todd's house in a small plane. ..........

**2**   **Listen and write the number.**

## 3 🔍 ✏️ Read and draw lines.

The baby is behind the door.
The mother is between the bed and the desk.
The clock is on the bookcase, between the books.
The lamp is on the desk.
The goat is on the desk, in front of the lamp.
There's a spider under the bed.

## 4 🎧 ✏️ Listen and complete. Chant.

| Whose | Which | ~~Who~~ | What | How many | Where | who | How old | What |
|---|---|---|---|---|---|---|---|---|

**1** _Who_ is that?
That's my brother, Paul.

**2** _____'s he doing?
He's catching a ball.

**3** _____ ball is it?
It's my cousin Nick's.

**4** _____ is he?
He's very young.
He's only six.

**5** _____ is he now?
He's in the hall.

**6** _____'s he doing?
He's throwing his ball.

**7** _____ balls have you got?
I don't know!
We've got a lot.

**8** _____ one's your favourite – red or blue?
I don't know!
And _____ are you?

53

# 9 Our clothes

**1** 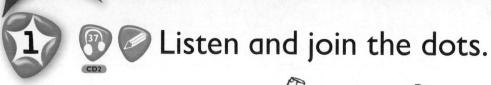 Listen and join the dots.

**2** Follow the 'clothes' words.

| watch | shoes | glasses | lizard | cake |
|-------|-------|---------|--------|------|
| meat | frog | socks | burger | sheep |
| hat | T-shirt | jeans | carrots | goat |
| trousers | ice cream | cow | bread | spider |
| dress | skirt | jacket | shirt | handbag |

How many clothes are there? _____

Write the 'animal' words. _____

Write the 'food' words. _____

## 3  Write the words and colour the picture.

| a | b | c | d | e | f | g | h | i | j | k | l | m |
|---|---|---|---|---|---|---|---|---|---|---|---|---|
| ☆ | ■ | ○ | ▭ | ◆ | ◧ | ● | ★ | ◈ | △ | ▼ | ⌣ | ◖ |

| n | o | p | q | r | s | t | u | v | w | x | y | z |
|---|---|---|---|---|---|---|---|---|---|---|---|---|
| ◭ | ✪ | ◸ | ◇ | ▲ | ◡ | ▽ | □ | ▬ | ◟ | ▽ | ▭ | ◹ |

I'm / \_ \_ \_ \_ \_ \_ \_ / \_ \_ \_ / \_ \_ \_ \_ \_ \_ \_ ,/ \_ /

\_ \_ \_ \_ \_ \_ \_ \_ / \_ \_ \_ \_ \_ \_ ,/ \_ \_ \_ \_ /

\_ \_ \_ \_ \_ \_ ,/ \_ \_ \_ \_ \_ \_ / \_ \_ \_ \_ \_ \_ /

☆◭▭/☆/◭◆⌣▲◆▭/★☆▽ .

\_ \_ \_ \_ / \_ / \_ \_ \_ / \_ \_ \_ / \_ \_ \_ .

## 4  Describe your clothes.

I'm wearing _____

_____

_____

_____

**Follow the lines. Complete the sentences**

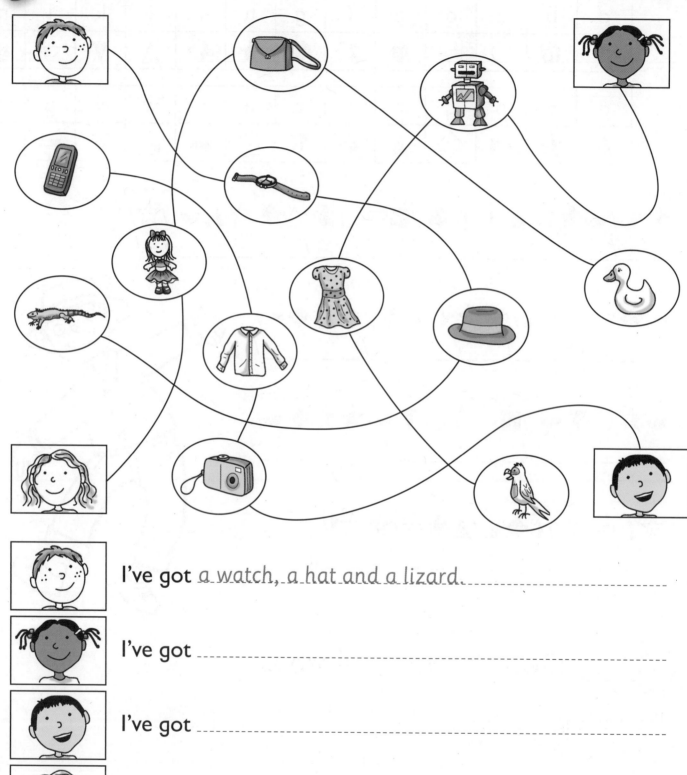

I've got a watch, a hat and a lizard.

I've got

I've got

I've got

**6**   **Ask your friends. Tick (✓).** (Have you got blue jeans?)

| Friends | blue jeans | brown shoes | a red jacket | a purple shirt | green socks | a black hat |
|---|---|---|---|---|---|---|
| **1** ............ | | | | | | |
| **2** ............ | | | | | | |
| **3** ............ | | | | | | |
| **4** ............ | | | | | | |
| **5** ............ | | | | | | |
| **6** ............ | | | | | | |

**Now colour the clothes and complete the graph.**

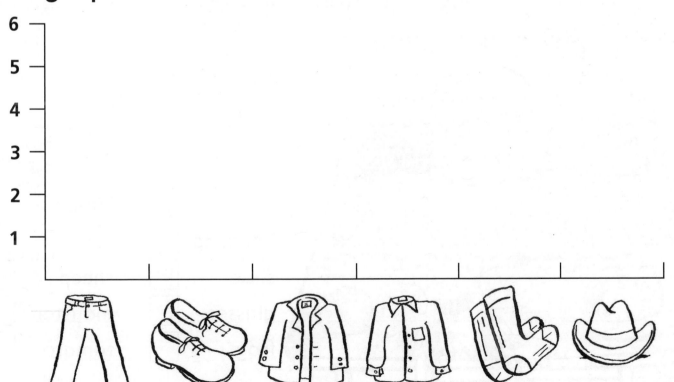

# Read and draw lines. ↓ ↘ →

**1**

| sock | frog | mouth |
|------|------|-------|
| brown | shop | cow |
| box | you | clock |

**2**

| shop | shirt | sock |
|------|-------|------|
| sheep | spider | skirt |
| shoe | street | show |

**3**

| girl | jump | guitar |
|------|------|--------|
| juice | jeans | jacket |
| green | garden | giraffe |

**4**

| teacher | clock | children |
|---------|-------|----------|
| which | clean | chicken |
| cat | chair | chips |

**8**  # Cross out five objects. Ask your friend.

 Have you got a hat?

 Yes, I have.

| hat | ✓ | lemon | ✓ |
|-----|---|-------|---|
| handbag | ✓ | cow | ✗ |
| shoe | ✗ | sheep | ✓ |
| glasses | ✓ | monster | ✗ |
| frog | ✗ | tomato | ✓ |

# My picture dictionary

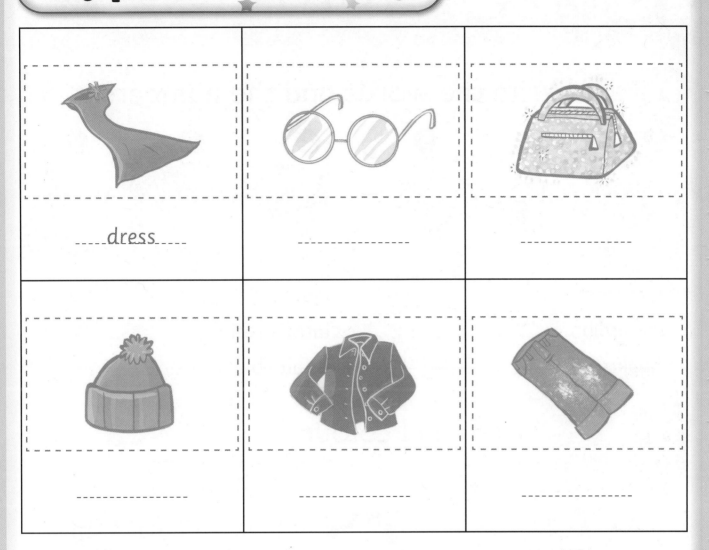

dress

59

# 10 Our hobbies

**1** ✏ Write the words and the numbers.

| ① | ② | ③ | ④ | ⑤ | ⑥ |

tapingin ...... *painting* ...... 4

nmaotdibn _____ ☐

cheyko _____ ☐

igatru _____ ☐

lateb ntesin _____ ☐

bslalaeb _____ ☐

**2** 🎧 50 CD2 ✏ Listen and colour.

## 3 Write the words.

**Down ↓**

1

2

3

5

7

8

**Across →**

3

4

6

7

9

10

## 4 Complete the sentences.

1 ↓ They're *playing* *table tennis.*

4 → They're ____________

5 ↓ She's ____________

6 → They're ____________ ____________

7 → She's ____________

9 → He's ____________

## 5 🎧 53 CD2 ✏️ Listen and tick (✓) or cross (✗) the boxes.

**1** **a** ☑️  **b** ☐  **c** ☐

**2** **a** ☐  **b** ☐  **c** ☐

**3** **a** ☐  **b** ☐  **c** ☐

**4** **a** ☐  **b** ☐  **c** ☐

## 6 ✏️ Draw and write about you.

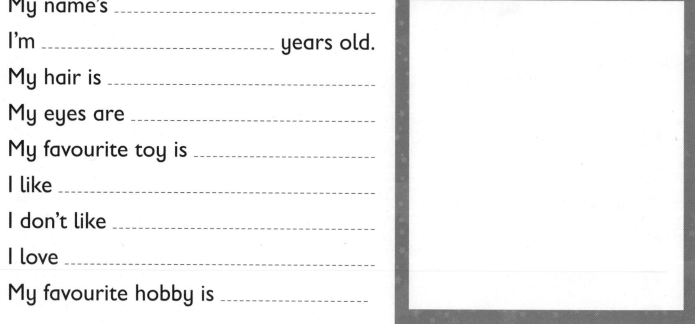

My name's _____

I'm _____ years old.

My hair is _____

My eyes are _____

My favourite toy is _____

I like _____

I don't like _____

I love _____

My favourite hobby is _____

# Choose. Tick (✓) or cross (✗) the boxes.

| | 🖌 | 🎸 | ⚾ | 🏑 | 🎣 | 🎾 | ⚽ | 🏊 |
|---|---|---|---|---|---|---|---|---|
| Ben | ✓ | ✓ | ✓ | ✓ | ✓ | ✗ | ✗ | ✗ |
| Ann | ✗ | ✗ | ✗ | ✗ | ✗ | ✓ | ✓ | ✓ |
| Nick | ✓ | ✗ | ✓ | ✗ | ✓ | ✓ | ✗ | ✗ |
| Sue | ✗ | ✓ | ✗ | ✓ | ✗ | ✗ | ✓ | ✓ |

## Now ask and answer questions.
## Tick (✓) or cross (✗) the boxes.

- Does Ben like painting?
- Yes, he does.
- Does Ben like playing football?
- No, he doesn't.

| | 🖌 | 🎸 | ⚾ | 🏑 | 🎣 | 🎾 | ⚽ | 🏊 |
|---|---|---|---|---|---|---|---|---|
| Ben | ✓ | ✓ | ✓ | ✗ | ✗ | ✗ | ✗ | ✗ |
| Ann | ✗ | ✓ | ✗ | ✗ | ✗ | ✗ | ✓ | ✓ |
| Nick | ✗ | ✗ | ✗ | ✗ | ✗ | ✗ | ✓ | ✗ |
| Sue | ✓ | ✓ | ✓ | ✓ | ✓ | ✗ | ✓ | ✓ |

**8** Listen and tick (✔) or cross (✗) the box.

**1** run ☐    one ✔    **6** game ☐    room ☐

**2** head ☐    red ☐    **7** number ☐    brother ☐

**3** write ☐    white ☐    **8** door ☐    draw ☐

**4** like ☐    ride ☐    **9** lorry ☐    sorry ☐

**5** rice ☐    mice ☐    **10** blue ☐    ruler ☐

  **9** Read. Write the words.

Hello. I'm Tom. Now, I'm at

_____school_____ . I'm playing

_____ . I'm wearing

a red _____ and

long blue _____ .

I like doing sport.

For lunch today I've got

some _____ and an

_____ . I like having

lunch at school.

badminton

Tick (✔) or cross (✗).

I can write 'sport' and 'hobby' words. ☐

I can talk about my likes. ☐

65

**1** ✏ Write the letters and the words.

_ _ u _ _ _ _                                      _ _ _ _ _ _ _ _

**2** 🔍✏ Find the different word.

| **1** tree | garden | flower | ~~car~~ |
| **2** shoe | camera | robot | kite |
| **3** sausage | armchair | chicken | fries |
| **4** lemonade | orange | milk | water |
| **5** badminton | basketball | soccer | bus |
| **6** café | desk | hospital | school |
| **7** cupboard | bed | sofa | kitchen |
| **8** kitchen | hall | bathroom | mirror |

## Listen and draw.

  ## Write the words.

me   you   her   it   us   ~~them~~

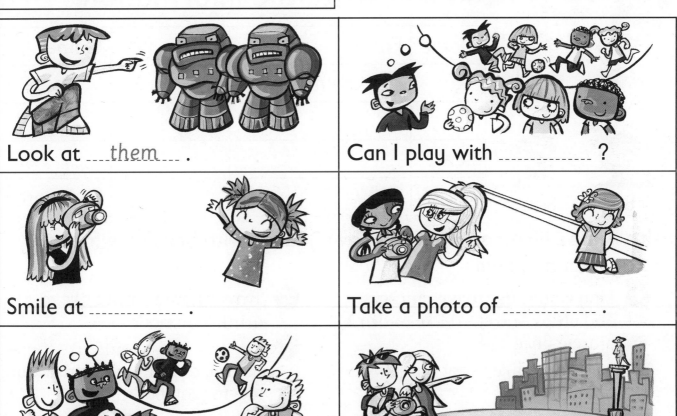

Look at ....them.... .

Can I play with _____ ?

Smile at _____ .

Take a photo of _____ .

Come and play with _____ .

Take a photo of _____ .

## 5 ✏ Write the sentences.

**1** ( fries? ) ( some ) ( Would ) ( like ) ( you )

**2** ( some ) ( please. ) ( cake, ) ( like ) ( I'd )

**3** ( Would ) ( like ) ( you ) ( to play ) ( us? ) ( with )

**4** ( to play ) ( I'd ) ( table tennis. ) ( like )

1  Would you like some fries?

2  ------------------------------------------------

3  ------------------------------------------------

4  ------------------------------------------------

## 6 🔍✏ Read and write the information.

 Anna  May

 Ben  Sam

| Name | Food | Drink | Game |
|------|------|-------|------|
| May | chicken and chips | | |
| | | water | |
| Ben | | | |
| | | | badminton |

It's Anna's birthday and she's having lunch with her three friends, May, Ben and Sam.

**1** May would like to eat chicken and chips and she'd like to drink orange juice.

**2** Ben would like to eat burgers and potatoes.

**3** One boy would like to eat sausages and tomatoes, and he'd like to drink water.

**4** Two children would like to drink lemonade.

**5** The two boys would like to play hockey and the two girls would like to play badminton.

**6** One girl would like to eat carrots and rice. It's her birthday today.

# ✏️ Choose and join.

# 💬✏️ Now ask and join.

What would Jill like?    She'd like fries.

**Follow the sound.**

| | | | | |
|---|---|---|---|---|
| c<u>ou</u>sin———b<u>u</u>t | p<u>ur</u>ple | n<u>u</u>mber | r<u>u</u>n |
| <u>ou</u>r | <u>u</u>nderstand | b<u>ou</u>nce | m<u>u</u>m | g<u>ui</u>tar |
| f<u>our</u> | c<u>u</u>pboard | y<u>our</u>s | l<u>u</u>nch | y<u>our</u> |
| m<u>ou</u>th | d<u>u</u>ck | j<u>ui</u>ce | <u>u</u>s | m<u>ou</u>se |
| r<u>u</u>ler | y<u>ou</u>ng | f<u>u</u>nny | j<u>u</u>mp | s<u>au</u>sage |
| b<u>ur</u>ger | h<u>ou</u>se | fr<u>ui</u>t | p<u>u</u>t | <u>ou</u>rs |

**9**   **Look at the sentence. Write words.**

Happy birthday, Simon.
It's your garden party.

_young_

## My picture dictionary

burger

## My progress

Tick (✓) or cross (✗).

I can ask for food and drink. ☐

I can talk about party food. ☐

71

## 1 Listen and tick (✓) the word. Find the words.

```
a s m o b s a n r
f h o l i d a y h
l e u t r e n g m
o l n i d f i s h
w l t s u n m e t
e m a g (s e a) f r
r u i h k h l o e
s a n d a r s t e
```

1 sea ✓    she ☐
2 song ☐    sun ☐
3 sand ☐    hand ☐
4 shell ☐    she ☐
5 mountain ☐    mouth ☐
6 three ☐    tree ☐
7 floors ☐    flowers ☐
8 bird ☐    big ☐
9 animals ☐    apples ☐
10 phone ☐    fish ☐
11 holiday ☐    today ☐

## 2 Match. Write the words.

| ho | ____hockey____ | ____holiday____ |
| sh | _____ | _____ |
| bea | _____ | _____ |
| tr | _____ | _____ |
| s | _____ | _____ |
| mou | _____ | |

ntain    ~~liday~~
se    irt
~~ckey~~    un
ees    ch
ell    ain
and    utiful

**3** **Listen and colour.**

  **4** **Look at the picture. Write the words.**

| sand   shells   sea   mountains   likes   ~~holiday~~   swimming |
|---|
| doesn't   beach |

Hello. My name's Nick. I'm on _holiday_ . I'm at the _____

with my family. It's great.

Today, I'm playing in the _____ with my brother. We love

_____ . My sister doesn't like swimming. She _____

walking on the yellow _____ and picking up _____ .

My mum and dad like the beach, but my grandfather _____

like holidays in the sun. He likes walking in the _____ .

He loves looking at the birds, the animals and the green trees.

**5** 🎧 ✏️ Listen and tick (✓) the box.

**1** What does Nick want to do?

a ☐  b ✓  c ☐

**2** What does Mary want to have for lunch?

a ☐  b ☐  c ☐

**3** What does Peter want for his birthday?

a ☐  b ☐  c ☐

**4** What does Susan want to drink?

a ☐  b ☐  c ☐

**5** What does Sally want to play?

a ☐  b ☐  c ☐

**6** Where does John want to go?

a ☐  b ☐  c ☐

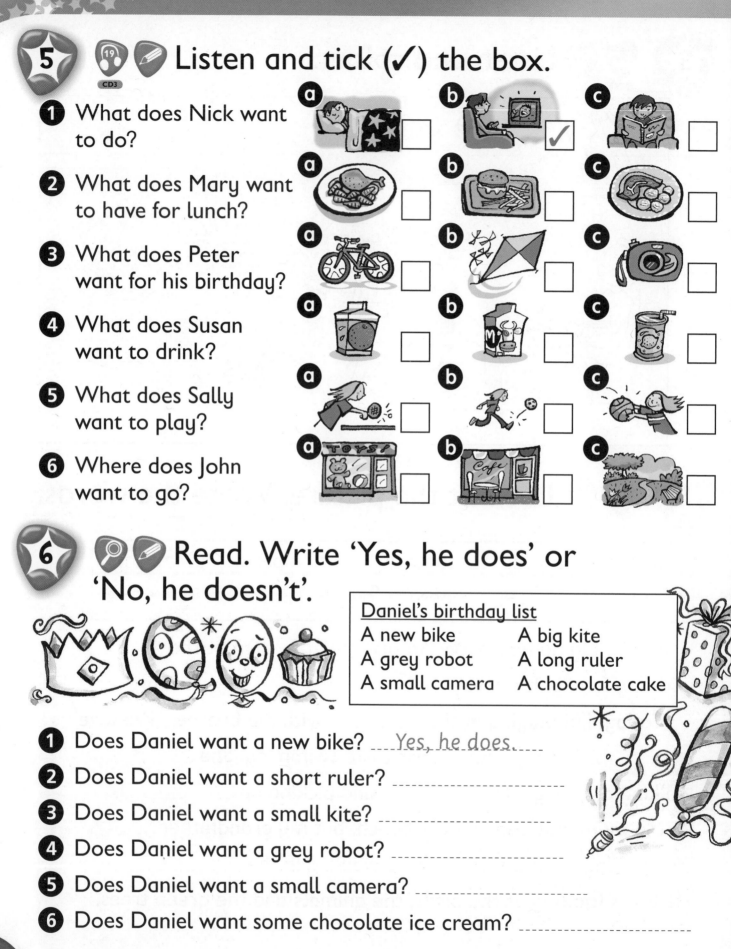

**6** 🔍 ✏️ Read. Write 'Yes, he does' or 'No, he doesn't'.

Daniel's birthday list
A new bike       A big kite
A grey robot     A long ruler
A small camera   A chocolate cake

**1** Does Daniel want a new bike? ....Yes, he does.....

**2** Does Daniel want a short ruler? _____

**3** Does Daniel want a small kite? _____

**4** Does Daniel want a grey robot? _____

**5** Does Daniel want a small camera? _____

**6** Does Daniel want some chocolate ice cream? _____

74

**7** ✏ **Write the words.**

| red | ~~yellow~~ | socks | bed | box |

I want ......_yellow_......

And you want _____

She wants an armchair

And he wants a _____

They want a jacket

And we want some _____

She wants a bag

And he wants a _____

**(23) Listen and chant.**
CD3

**8** ✏ **Answer the questions.**

**1** How many people are there? _There are four people._____

**2** What's the man drinking? _____

**3** What's the woman doing? _____

**4** Is the dog walking? _____

**5** Where's the boy swimming? _____

**6** What's the girl picking up? _____

**7** How many birds are there? _____

**8** What are the birds doing? _____

**9** Find the different sound.

**1** s<u>h</u>irt   s<u>h</u>oe   s<u>h</u>eep   ~~sock~~

**2** <u>y</u>ou   <u>j</u>uice   <u>y</u>oung   <u>y</u>ellow

**3** <u>j</u>ump   l<u>u</u>nch   r<u>u</u>ler   tr<u>u</u>ck

**4** <u>r</u>ed   l<u>e</u>g   <u>w</u>rite   <u>r</u>obot

**5** st<u>o</u>p   <u>o</u>n   cl<u>o</u>ck   <u>o</u>ne

**6** <u>j</u>eans   <u>y</u>es   <u>g</u>iraffe   <u>j</u>acket

**7** b<u>u</u>rger   r<u>u</u>n   n<u>u</u>mber   <u>u</u>gly

**8** sh<u>o</u>p   fr<u>o</u>g   l<u>o</u>rry   s<u>o</u>fa

 **10**  Complete the questions. Then answer.

| ugly   old   new   short   ~~small~~   dirty |

**1** Is your kitchen big or _____ *small* _____ ?

_____

**2** Is your city beautiful or _____ ?

_____

**3** Is your street long or _____ ?

_____

**4** Is your bedroom clean or _____ ?

_____

**5** Is your bed new or _____ ?

_____

**6** Is your school old or _____ ?

_____

# My picture dictionary

sand

# My progress

Tick (✓) or cross (✗).

I can talk about my holidays. ☐

I can say what I want. ☐

**1** 🔍 ✏️ **Look at page 78 of the Pupil's Book. Write the answers.**

**1** What's Jill cleaning? ....*She's cleaning the beach.*....

**2** Can the birds swim? _____

**3** What does Jill want? _____

**4** Is Sue a doctor? _____

**5** Where's Sue? _____

**6** What's Sue doing? _____

**7** Where are the children? _____

**8** What are the children doing? _____

**9** How old's Julie? _____

**10** What's Julie doing? _____

 **2** 🎧28 CD3 ✏️ **Listen and colour.**

## 3 ✏️ Write the words in alphabetical order.

........apple........    ........bread........    .................... .......................

.................... .................... .................... .......................

.................... .................... .................... .......................

.................... ....................

## 4 ✏️ Write the words. Change one letter.

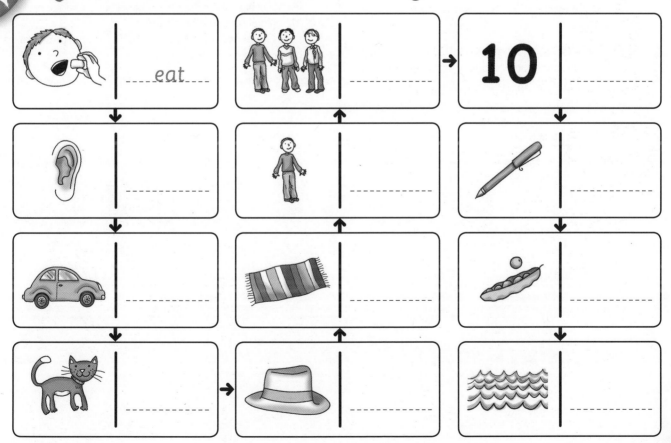

# Thanks and Acknowledgements

## Authors' thanks

Many thanks to everyone at Cambridge University Press and in particular to:

Maria Pylas for supervising the whole project and for her unfailing good humour and support;

Susan Norris for her unflagging energy, sound editorial judgement and constant enthusiasm;

Emily Hird and Liane ('there's just one little thing ...') Grainger for all their hard work and enthusiasm;

Thanks to Mel Sharp for her wonderfully inspired and inspiring illustrations and to Melanie Williams for doing such a great job on the Teacher's Books.

And last but not least, our heartfelt thanks to Hilary Ratcliff for her sharp-eyed observations and excellent suggestions throughout the whole project and, most especially, for her skilful editing of the Teacher's Book of this cycle.

We would also like to thank all our pupils and colleagues at Star English, El Palmar, Murcia and especially Jim Kelly and Julie Woodman for their help and suggestions at various stages of the project.

## Dedications

This is for my friends, Maribel Salcedo, Carmen Sánchez, Victoria Gómez and Maria Noguera, for their luminosity. – CN

To my great friends in England, who always receive us so kindly, offering their warmth and friendship: Mike and Nicola, Shaun and Lorraine and The Wheelers. – MT

The authors and publishers would like to thank the following consultants for their invaluable feedback:

Coralyn Bradshaw, Pippa Mayfield, Hilary Ratcliff, Melanie Williams.

We would also like to thank all the teachers who allowed us to observe their classes, and who gave up their invaluable time for interviews and focus groups.

The authors and publishers are grateful to the following illustrators:

Melanie Sharp, c/o Sylvie Poggio; Gary Swift; Lisa Williams, c/o Sylvie Poggio; Emily Skinner, c/o Graham-Cameron Illustration; Chris Garbutt, c/o Arena.

The authors and publishers would like to thank the children at St Matthew's Primary School, Cambridge, for participating so enthusiastically in the photograph sessions.

The publishers are grateful to the following contributors:

Pentacorbig: cover design, book design and page make-up
Melanie Sharp: cover illustration
John Green and Tim Woolf, TEFL Tapes: audio recordings
Robert Lee: song writing